easy GUITAR play along

ROCK N' ROLL

ISBN 978-1-4584-1613-1

HAL•LEONARD® CORPORATION

7777 W. BLUEMOUND RD. P.O. BOX 13819 MILWAUKEE, WI 53213

Visit Hal Leonard Online at
www.halleonard.com

GUITAR NOTATION LEGEND

THE MUSICAL STAFF shows pitches and rhythms and is divided by bar lines into measures. Pitches are named after the first seven letters of the alphabet.

TABLATURE graphically represents the guitar fingerboard. Each horizontal line represents a string, and each number represents a fret.

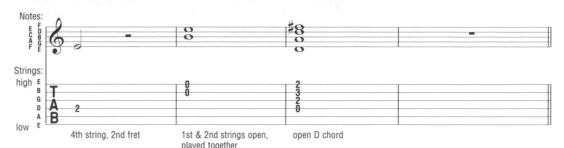

4th string, 2nd fret   1st & 2nd strings open,   open D chord
played together

HALF-STEP BEND: Strike the note and bend up 1/2 step.

WHOLE-STEP BEND: Strike the note and bend up one step.

GRACE NOTE BEND: Strike the note and immediately bend up as indicated.

SLIGHT (MICROTONE) BEND: Strike the note and bend up 1/4 step.

BEND AND RELEASE: Strike the note and bend up as indicated, then release back to the original note. Only the first note is struck.

PRE-BEND: Bend the note as indicated, then strike it.

VIBRATO: The string is vibrated by rapidly bending and releasing the note with the fretting hand.

PALM MUTING: The note is partially muted by the pick hand lightly touching the string(s) just before the bridge.

HAMMER-ON: Strike the first (lower) note with one finger, then sound the higher note (on the same string) with another finger by fretting it without picking.

PULL-OFF: Place both fingers on the notes to be sounded. Strike the first note and without picking, pull the finger off to sound the second (lower) note.

LEGATO SLIDE: Strike the first note and then slide the same fret-hand finger up or down to the second note. The second note is not struck.

SHIFT SLIDE: Same as legato slide, except the second note is struck.

TRILL: Very rapidly alternate between the notes indicated by continuously hammering on and pulling off.

TAPPING: Hammer ("tap") the fret indicated with the pick-hand index or middle finger and pull off to the note fretted by the fret hand.

NATURAL HARMONIC: Strike the note while the fret-hand lightly touches the string directly over the fret indicated.

PINCH HARMONIC: The note is fretted normally and a harmonic is produced by adding the edge of the thumb or the tip of the index finger of the pick hand to the normal pick attack.

TREMOLO PICKING: The note is picked as rapidly and continuously as possible.

VIBRATO BAR DIVE AND RETURN: The pitch of the note or chord is dropped a specified number of steps (in rhythm), then returned to the original pitch.

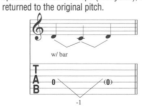

VIBRATO BAR SCOOP: Depress the bar just before striking the note, then quickly release the bar.

VIBRATO BAR DIP: Strike the note and then immediately drop a specified number of steps, then release back to the original pitch.

Additional Musical Definitions

(accent) • Accentuate note (play it louder).

(staccato) • Play the note short.

D.S. al Coda • Go back to the sign (𝄋), then play until the measure marked "*To Coda*," then skip to the section labelled "**Coda**."

D.C. al Fine • Go back to the beginning of the song and play until the measure marked "***Fine***" (end).

Fill • Label used to identify a brief melodic figure which is to be inserted into the arrangement.

N.C. • Harmony is implied.

• Repeat measures between signs.

• When a repeated section has different endings, play the first ending only the first time and the second ending only the second time.

Blue Suede Shoes

Words and Music by Carl Lee Perkins

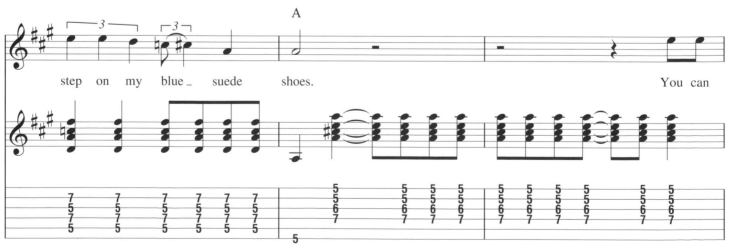

do an-y-thing,— but lay off——— of my blue— suede shoes.

%̸ Verse

1. Well, you can knock me down,— step in my face,—
2. *See additional lyrics*

slan-der my name— all —— o-ver the place,— and do an-y-thing ——— that you

wan-na do,— but uh-uh, hon-ey, lay off——— of my shoes, and don't——

Chorus

— you step on my blue suede shoes. You can

do an‑y‑thing, _ but lay off _ of my blue _ suede shoes.

To Coda 1 ⊕
Guitar Solo

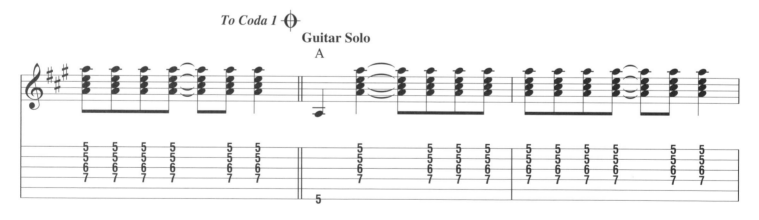

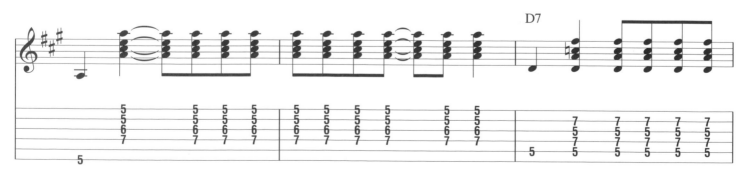

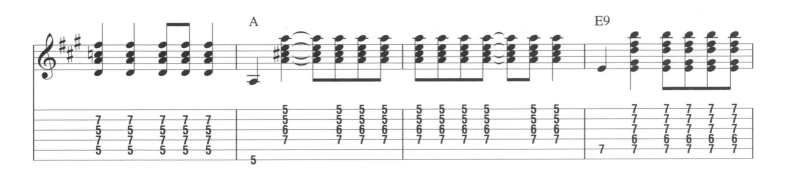

D.S. al Coda 1

2. Well, you   can

⊕ Coda 1
Guitar Solo

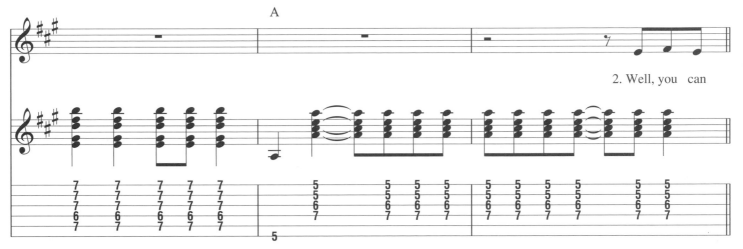

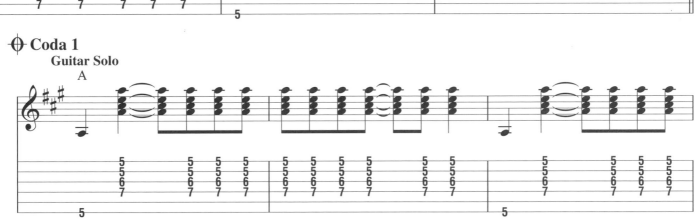

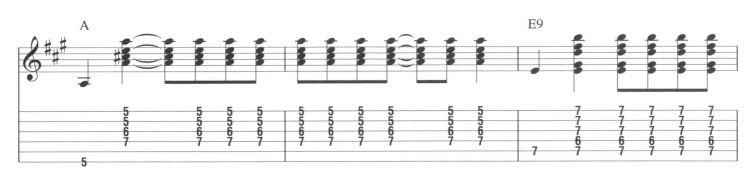

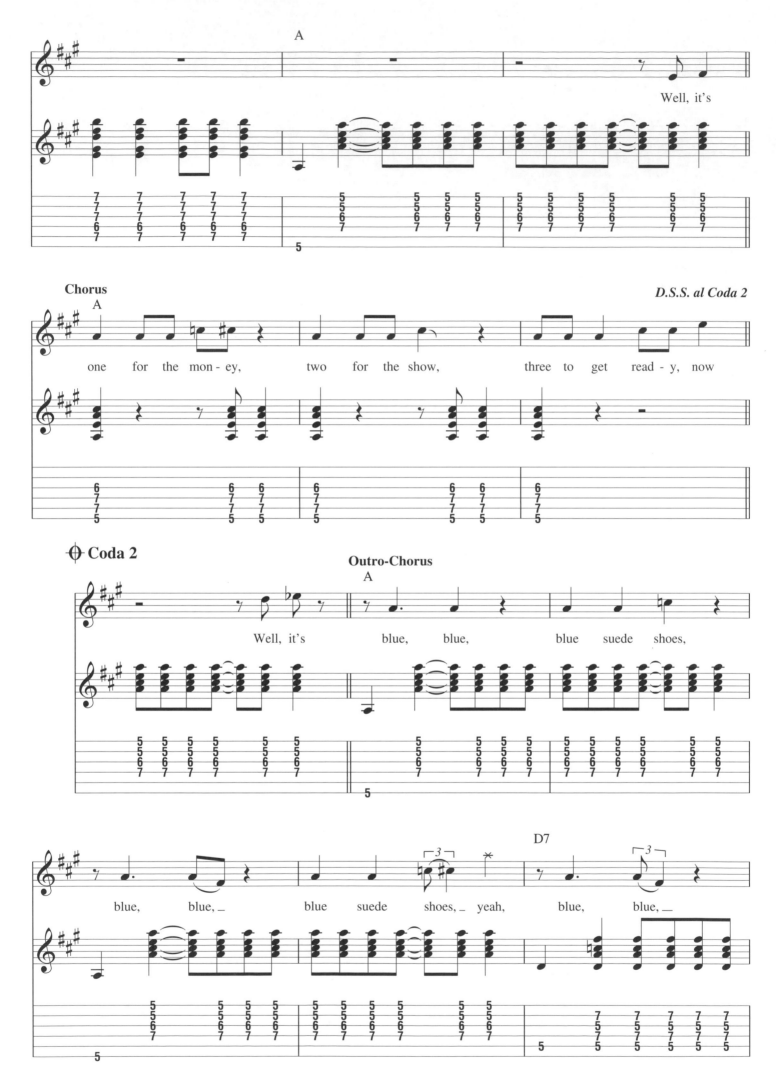

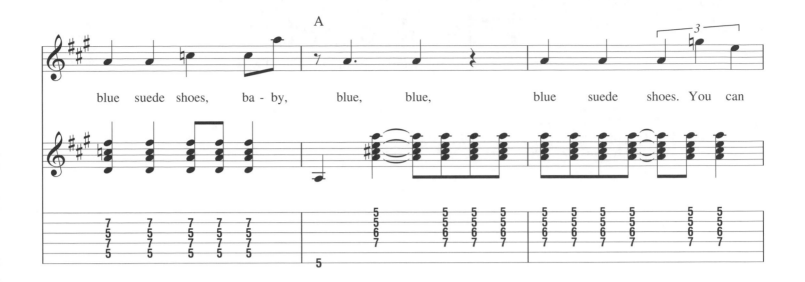

blue suede shoes, ba - by, blue, blue, blue suede shoes. You can

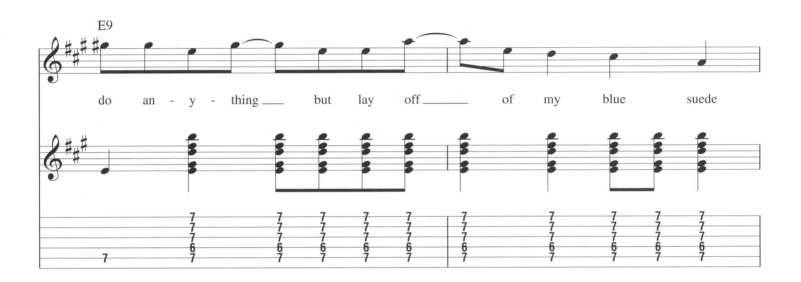

do an - y - thing ____ but lay off _____ of my blue suede

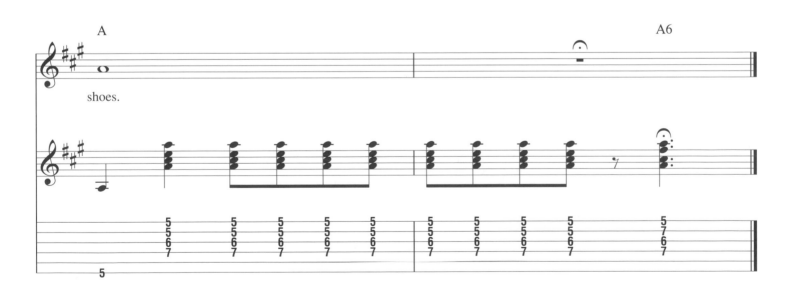

shoes.

Additional Lyrics

2. Well, you can burn my house, steal my car,
   Drink my liquor from an old fruit jar,
   And do anything that you wanna do,
   But uh-oh, honey, lay off of them shoes,
   And don't you...

I Get Around

Words and Music by Brian Wilson and Mike Love

Intro
Moderately fast ♩ = 148
N.C.

Oo.

(Round, round, get a-round, I get a-round, _yeah. Get a-round, round, round,

w/ clean tone

% Chorus
G5

_ I get a-round _____ from town to town. _

I get a-round.) _ (Get a-round, round, round, I get a-round. _

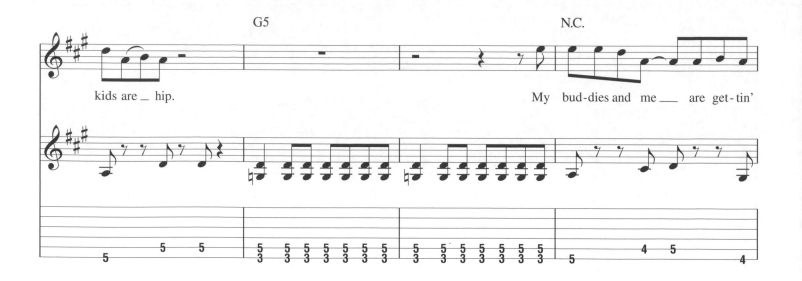

kids are _ hip.

My bud-dies and me _ are get-tin'

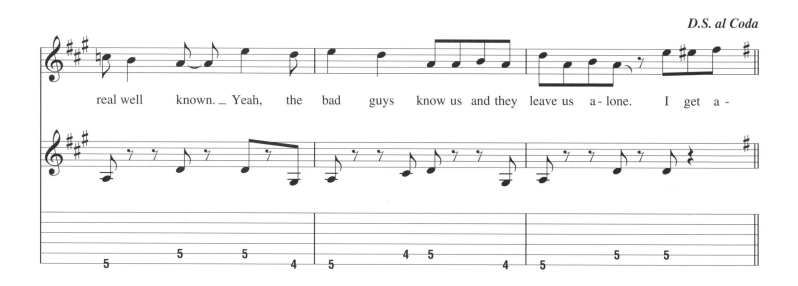

D.S. al Coda

real well known. _ Yeah, the bad guys know us and they leave us a-lone. I get a-

Coda

Get a-round, round, round.

I get a-round. _ I get a - round.) _____

(Round.) _____

14

15

would-n't be right to leave your best girl home on a Sat - ur - day night. I get a-

Chorus

round _____ from town to town. _

(Get a-round, round, round, I get a - round. _ Get a-round, round, round,

I'm a real cool head. _____ I'm mak-in' real good bread. _

I get a-round. _ Get a-round, round, round, I get a - round. _

I'm a Believer

Words and Music by Neil Diamond

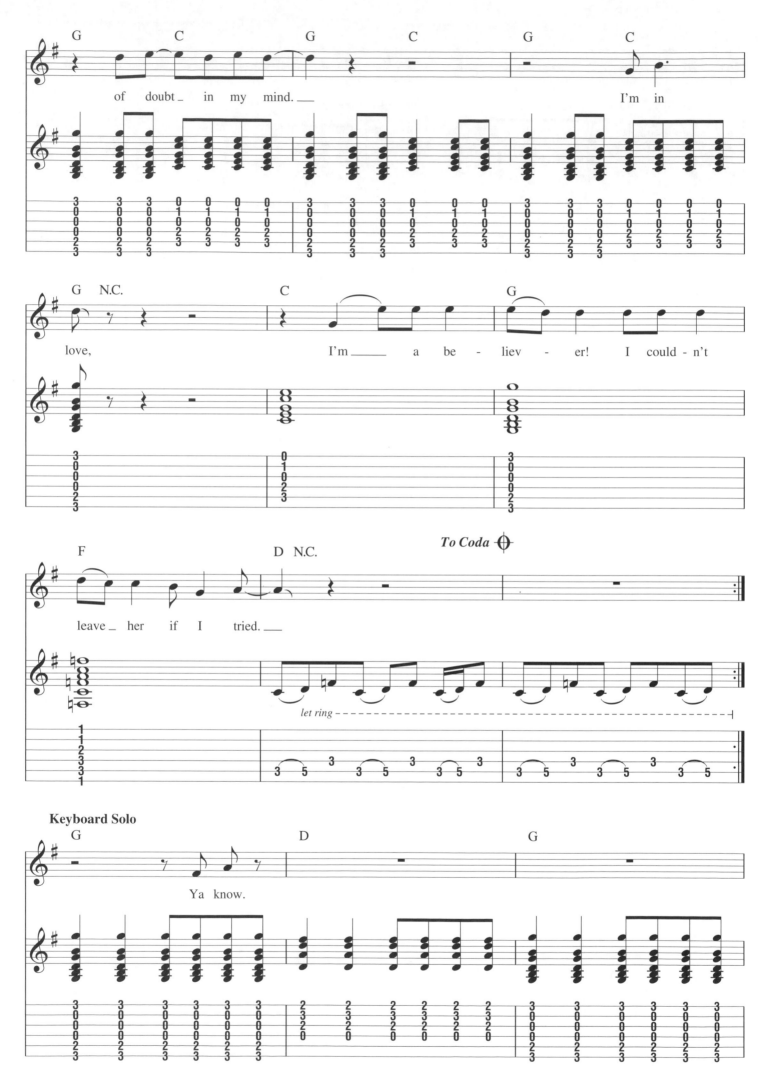

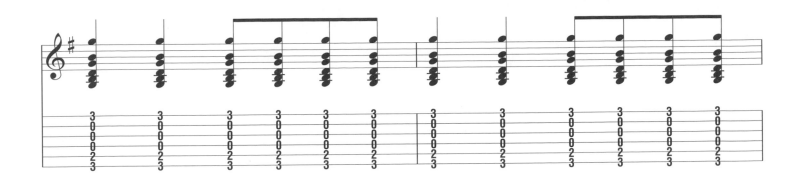

D.S. al Coda

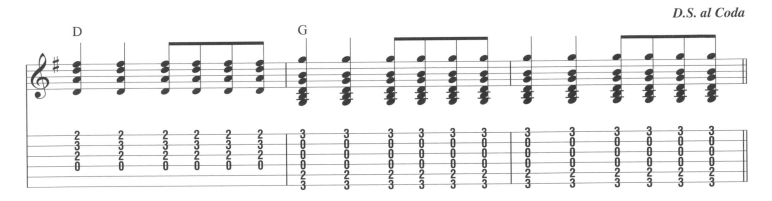

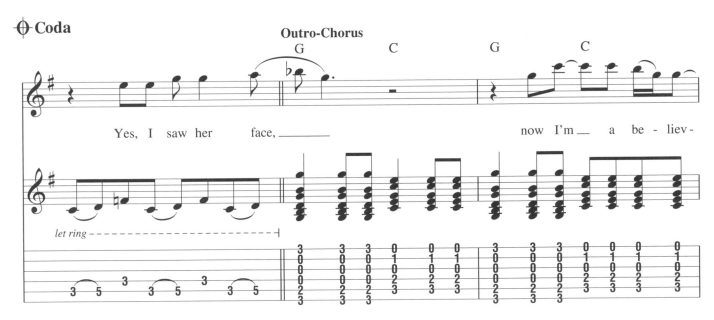

⊕ Coda

Outro-Chorus

Yes, I saw her face, _____ now I'm __ a be - liev-

let ring - - - - - - - - - - - - - - - -

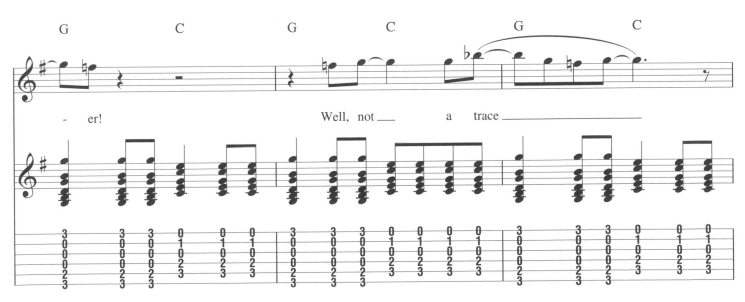

- er! Well, not __ a trace _____

Additional Lyrics

2. I thought love was more or less a givin' thing.
   Seems the more I gave, the less I got.

Pre-Chorus 2. What's the use in tryin'?
   All you get is pain.
   When I needed sunshine, I got rain.

Jailhouse Rock

Words and Music by Jerry Leiber and Mike Stoller

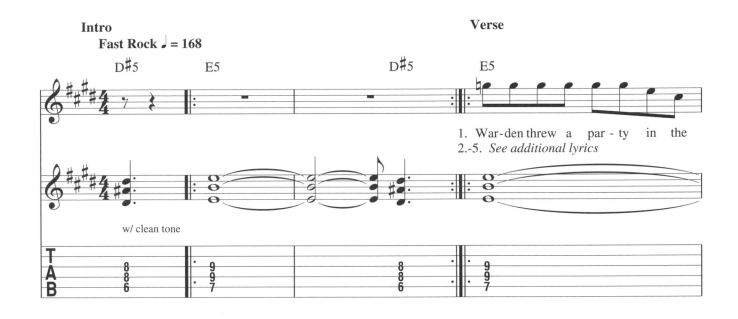

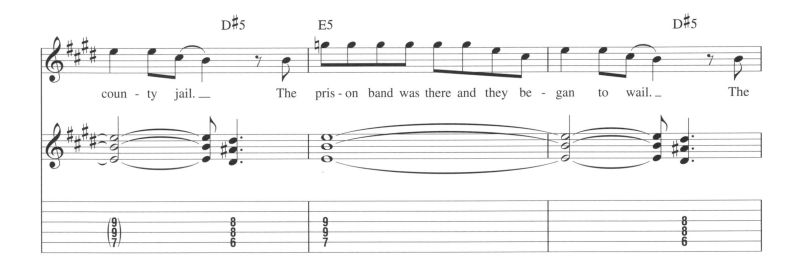

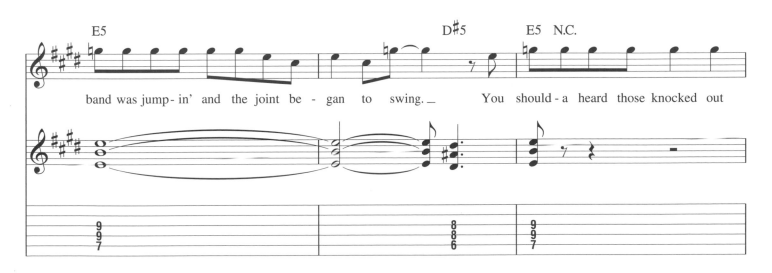

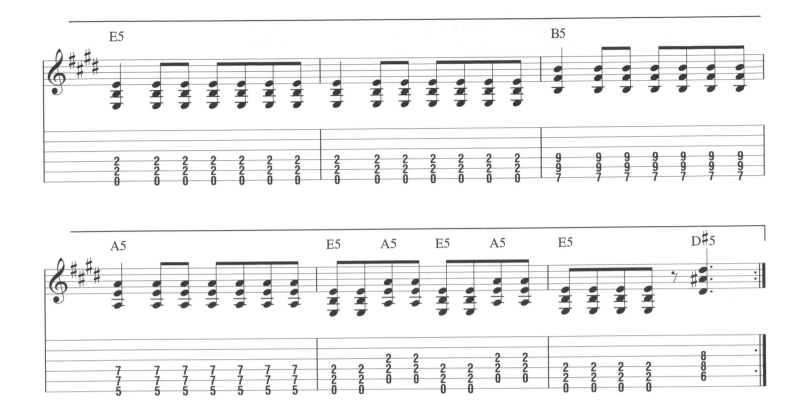

Additional Lyrics

2. Spider Murphy played the tenor saxophone.
   Little Joe was blowin' on the slide trombone.
   The drummer boy from Illinois went crash, boom, bang!
   The whole rhythm section was the Purple Gang.

3. Number forty-seven said to number three,
   "You the cutest jailbird I ever did see,
   I sure would be delighted with your company.
   Come on and do the Jailhouse Rock with me."

4. Sad Sack was sittin' on a block of stone,
   Way over in the corner weepin' all alone.
   The warden said, "Hey, buddy, don't you be no square.
   If you can't find a partner use a wooden chair."

5. Shifty Henry said to Bugs, "For heaven's sake,
   No one's lookin', now's our chance to make a break."
   Bugs, he turned to Shifty and he said, "Nix, nix,
   I wanna stick around awhile to get my kicks."

Oh, Pretty Woman

Words and Music by Roy Orbison and Bill Dees

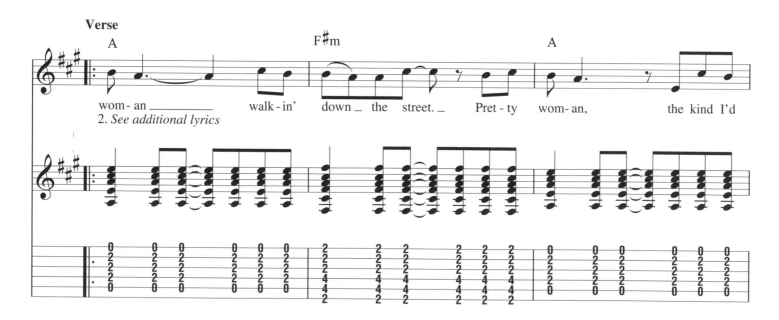

Bridge

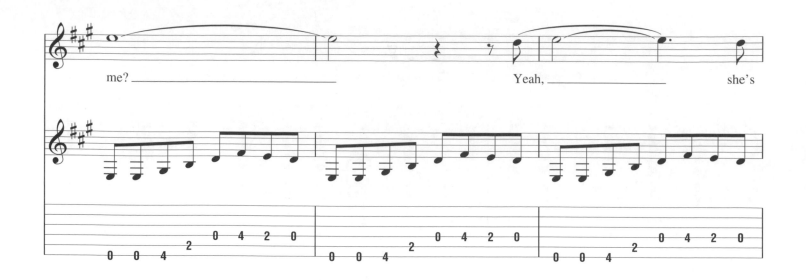

me? _____ Yeah, _____ she's

walk - in' ___ back to me. _____

Oh, _____ whoa, pret - ty wom - an.

Additional Lyrics

2. Pretty woman, won't you pardon me?
   Pretty woman, I couldn't help but see;
   Pretty woman, that you look lovely as can be.
   Are you lonely just like me?

Peggy Sue

Words and Music by Jerry Allison, Norman Petty and Buddy Holly

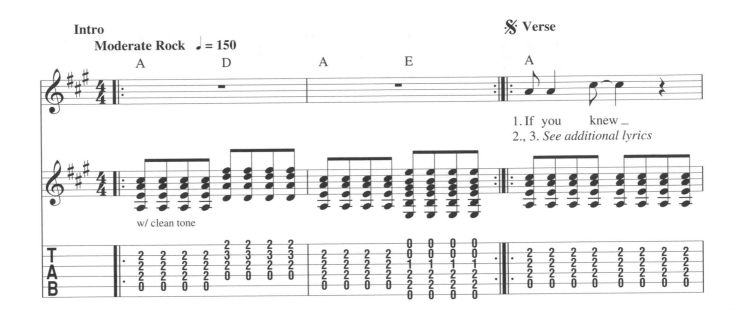

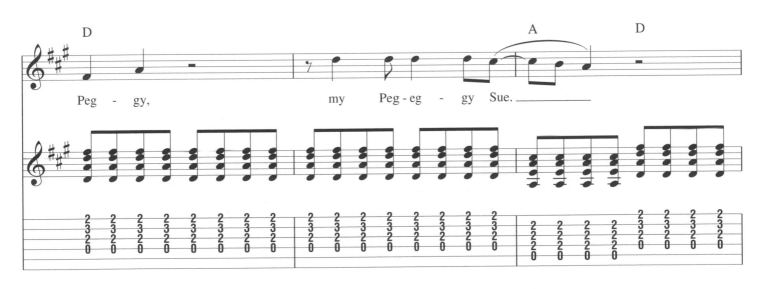

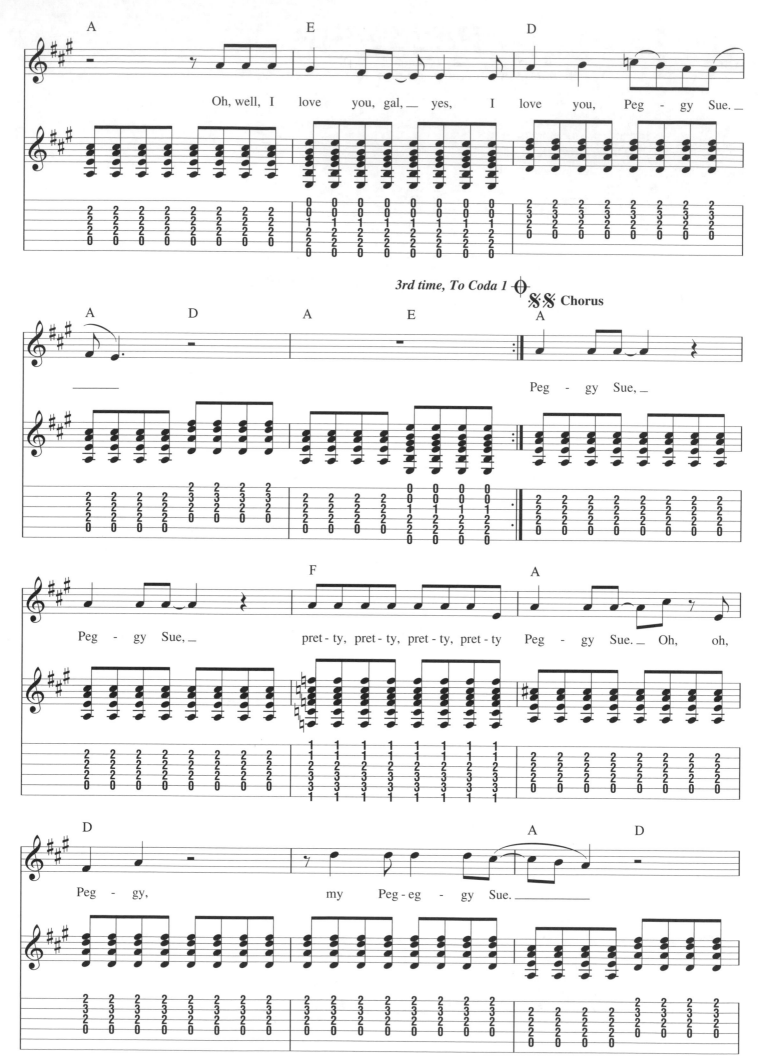

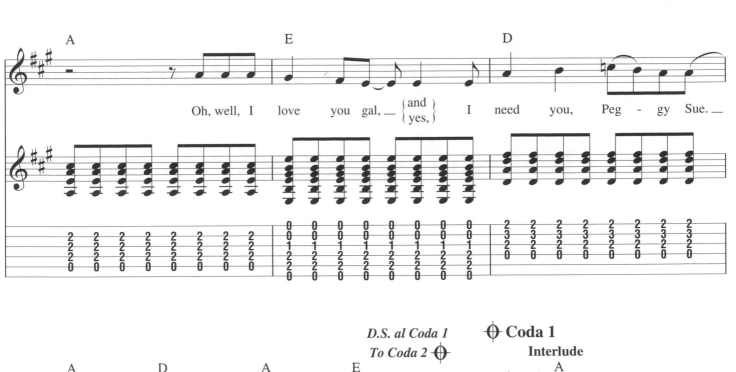

Oh, well, I love you gal, — {and} {yes,} I need you, Peg - gy Sue. —

D.S. al Coda 1
To Coda 2 ⊕

⊕ **Coda 1**

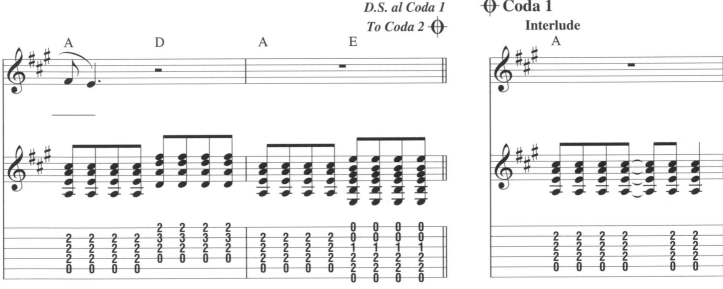

Interlude

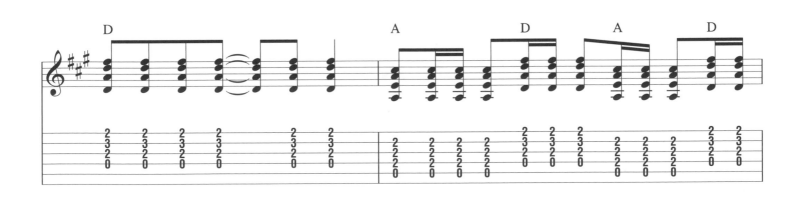

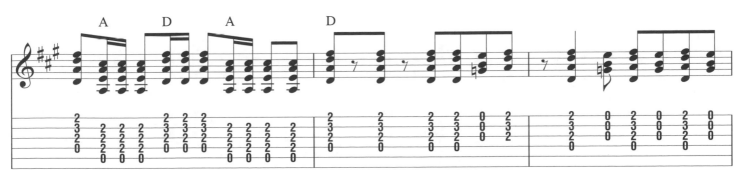

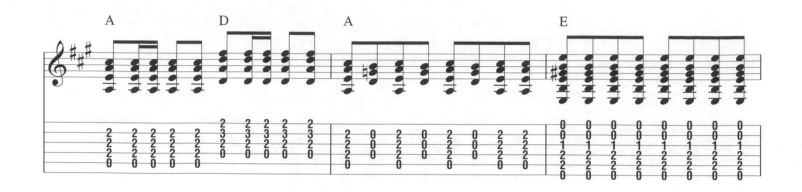

D.S.S. al Coda 2

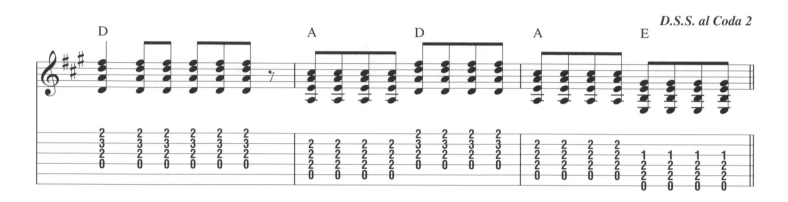

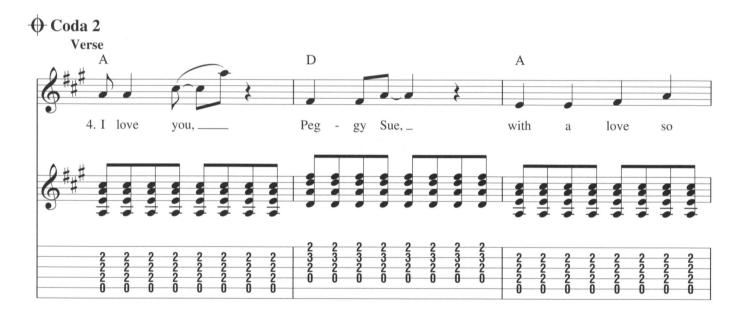

Coda 2

Verse

4. I love you, _____ Peg - gy Sue, _ with a love so

rare and true. _ Oh, oh, Peg - gy, my Peg - gy Sue -

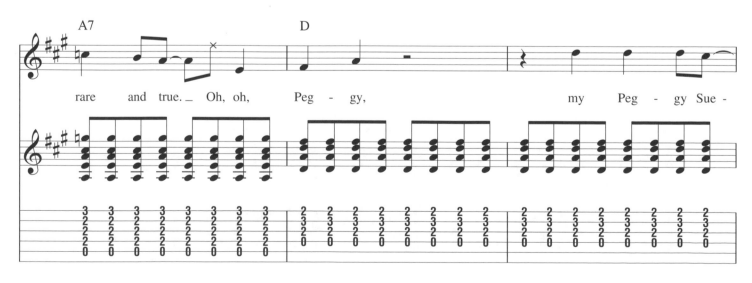

Additional Lyrics

2. Peggy Sue, Peggy Sue,
   Oh, how my heart yearns for you.
   Oh, Peggy, my Peggy Sue.
   Oh, well, I love you, gal.
   Yes, I love you, Peggy Sue.

3. I love you, Peggy Sue,
   With a love so rare and true.
   Oh, Peggy, my Peggy Sue.
   Well, I love you, gal.
   I want you, Peggy Sue.

Runaway

Words and Music by Del Shannon and Max Crook

Additional Lyrics

And as I still walk on I think of
The things we've done together,
Uh, while our hearts were young.

Wake Up Little Susie

Words and Music by Boudleaux Bryant and Felice Bryant

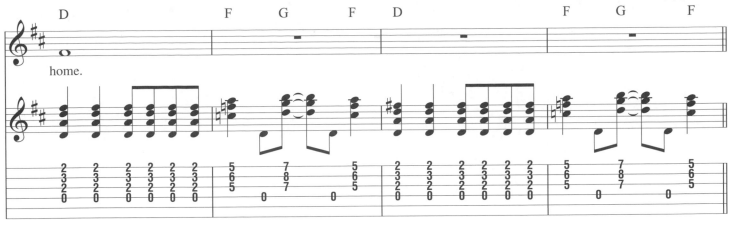

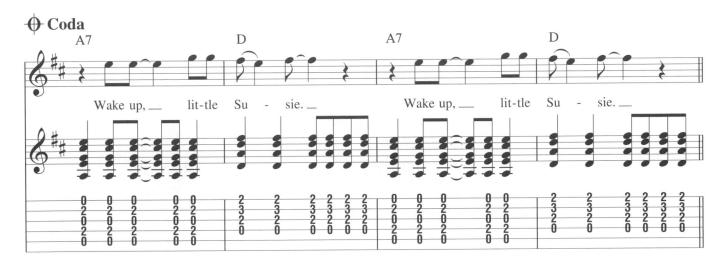

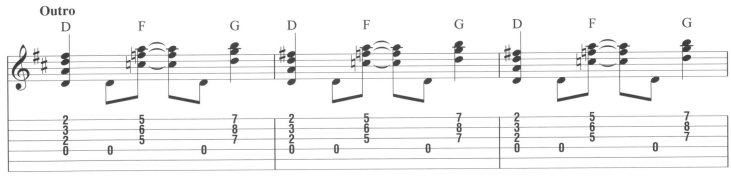

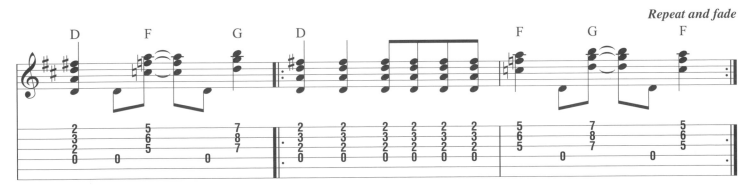

Additional Lyrics

3. Wake up, little Susie, wake up.
   Wake up, little Susie, wake up.
   The movie wasn't so hot,
   It didn't have much of a plot.
   We fell asleep, our goose is cooked,
   Our reputation is shot.
   Wake up, little Susie.
   Wake up, little Susie.

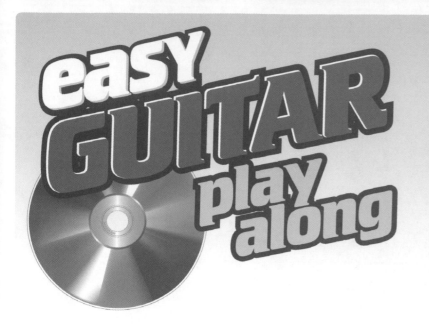

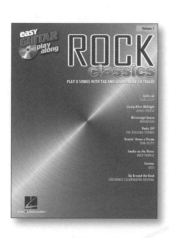
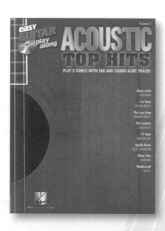
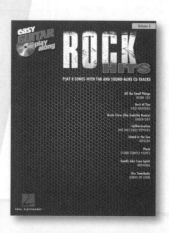